P9-CDW-208

759.13   12653
J-709
Wal

Walker, Lou Ann
  Roy Lichenstein: the
artist at work

ROY LICHTENSTEIN

The Artist at Work

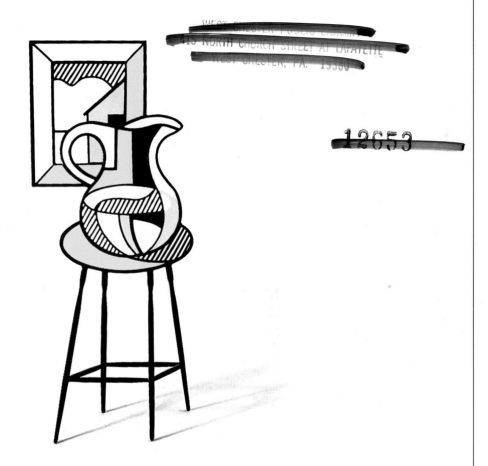

WEST CHESTER PUBLIC LIBRARY
415 NORTH CHURCH STREET AT LAFAYETTE
WEST CHESTER, PA. 19380

12653

BY LOU ANN WALKER

PHOTOGRAPHS BY MICHAEL ABRAMSON

DUTTON ▪ LODESTAR BOOKS ▪ NEW YORK

for my daughter, Kate
L.A.W.

in memory of my father, Philip
M.A.

———————

Text copyright © 1994 by Lou Ann Walker
Photographs copyright © 1994 by Michael Abramson
Artworks copyright © by Roy Lichtenstein
All rights reserved.

Library of Congress Cataloging-in-Publication Data

Walker, Lou Ann.
  Roy Lichtenstein: the artist at work / by Lou Ann Walker;
photographs by Michael Abramson. – 1st ed.
    p. cm.
  Summary: Discusses the work of pop artist Roy
Lichtenstein and describes how he develops a painting from
original idea to finished piece.
  ISBN 0-525-67435-7
  1. Lichtenstein, Roy, 1923-   –Criticism and
interpretation – Juvenile literature. [1. Lichtenstein, Roy,
1923-   2. Artists. 3. Art appreciation.] I. Abramson,
Michael. II. Title
N6537. L5W38 1994
709' . 2 – dc20
                                              93-2631
                                                 CIP
                                                  AC

Published in the United States by Lodestar Books,
an affiliate of Dutton Children's Books,
a division of Penguin Books USA Inc.,
375 Hudson Street, New York, New York 10014

Published simultaneously in Canada
by McClelland & Stewart, Toronto

Editor: Virginia Buckley
Designer: Wendy Palitz

Printed in Hong Kong
First Edition 10 9 8 7 6 5 4 3 2 1

———————

**Title page: *Picture and Pitcher,*
1977, is a visual pun.**

AN ARTIST'S BUSY LIFE

Roy Lichtenstein's studio is an artist's wonderland. As you enter, there are armies of easels and fat pots of bright-colored paints. The ceilings are more than twenty feet high. The walls look as if they are striped; long, wooden beams hold the many oversized paintings he's doing at any given time. The wide-planked floors are spattered with paint: splotches of blue and yellow, some pink and white here, red way over there.

When Roy walks into his studio each morning, he is very enthusiastic about what he's going to do that day. He is a trim man of medium height who stands very straight. Most days, he wears a T-shirt, blue jeans, and sneakers. On his wrist is a pink-faced watch with a bright green band. Often, as he talks, he runs his hand through his hair to brush it off his forehead.

The summer studio is in Southampton, New York, on the Atlantic Ocean beach. It's a squarish building, painted white inside and out.

There aren't many windows in the walls because Roy needs all the space he has to hang his many large-sized paintings. There are skylights through the roof. Even if the electricity is out because of a storm or hurricane—and that sometimes happens—the studio is washed evenly in light.

Roy Lichtenstein burst onto the art world scene around 1961 with a style that had never been used by serious painters. He took printing techniques from newspapers, especially comic strips. Because his oil paintings had flat, primary colors, Benday dots, and diagonal lines instead of brushstrokes, the pictures seemed cold.

Benday dots

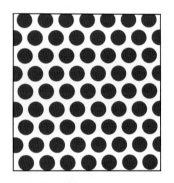

Diagonal lines

He even put cartoon characters into his drawings. People were shocked! Some observers couldn't tell whether or not he was just making an elaborate joke. At first, art critics said Roy Lichtenstein's work would be forgotten right away. They insisted that the public and art collectors would ignore Roy's paintings, or think they were silly. Instead, people enjoyed what they saw. The critics soon changed their minds.

Now Roy Lichtenstein is one of the most famous artists of our century. Cities and big companies around the world ask, or commission, Roy to create important paintings and sculptures for them. In the lobby of a New York City office building, an enormous, several-stories-tall painting, *Mural with Blue Brushstroke,* is an excellent example of how Roy's art has become part of many people's everyday lives. His work is found in permanent collections at every museum in the world that has modern art. And recently, the entire rotunda of the Guggenheim Museum in New York was given over to a major retrospective of his art. The exhibition of drawings, paintings, and sculptures from all stages of Roy's art

Collage of *Mural with Blue Brushstroke,* 1986

is to travel to Los Angeles, Montreal, and Europe.

But how does a painter like Roy go about creating his art? Where does he get his ideas? Few of us ever have a chance to watch firsthand how the artworks we see in a museum grow from an idea to a sketch to a full-fledged painting. It is a surprisingly exciting process. By visiting Roy Lichtenstein in his studio, we can see that creativity requires hard work. Here is an inside look at an artist's daily life.

For artist Roy Lichtenstein, the creative process is a crucial part of his life.

WORK IN PROGRESS

Classical music fills the studio as Roy climbs up on a tall ladder to study his drawing more closely. "I'm just looking this over," he says. He erases a line, then lifts a piece of tape to change the way it is placed. "The thing that makes my work look mechanical is that I'm using tape," he says. "The fact that I'm placing it rather freely is not obvious to the viewer. I like that contradiction."

He is a perfectionist. He wants the drawing to be absolutely right before he proceeds to the next step. It is fascinating to watch Roy because he constantly experiments. He is part scientist, part mathematician, part printer as he tries new things.

His technique is intriguing. Roy starts with a sketch on paper. Sometimes he uses a regular number 2 writing pencil, which gives a fuzzy line, or he chooses a drawing pencil, which gives a cleaner line. Getting the drawing right is a very important part of the process. He erases and changes the drawing until it is exactly the way he wants it. He may redraw the picture using tracing paper. He often colors in the picture with colored pencils so that he begins to get an idea of the way the final artwork will look.

A magic moment in the artist's studio as Roy stands before a clean canvas.

At this stage, he takes a piece of tracing paper, on which he outlines his pencil drawing with black India ink. This is the first step in making a collage, which is an assembly made by pasting various materials on a single surface. For his collage, Roy cuts out pieces of paper that have been painted the color he wants for the final artwork and pastes them to his drawing. He cuts the papers into precise— and sometimes very unusual—shapes. At this point, he also adds the distinctive dots and diagonal lines that are his trademark. During

these various stages, he continues his many experiments. "I reject a hundred images for every one I pick," Roy says.

Sometimes he chooses quiet, subtle colors. Other times, he likes his color combinations to be "screaming"—yellow and green next to red dots, for example. He also likes to vary the placement of objects and colors. Most viewers look at the center of a painting first, but in order to startle them, Roy might put a splash of yellow at the top of the painting.

For an important work, he might create several collages until the composition seems just right to him. When Roy is done with the final painting, it looks very much like this miniature composition.

His next step is to project that collage onto a wall. "I'm seeing what size I think the painting has to be," he says. "I measure that and order a canvas and stretch it." He prefers cotton duck for the canvas.

In laying out his work, Roy the artist is also part engineer and part scientist.

Once the canvas is stretched, it is undercoated with white paint. The work has to be done very carefully so that no dirt gets into the paint. The surface must be absolutely smooth.

He again uses the projector to throw the image of the collage onto the stretched canvas. "Next, I draw that image on the canvas," Roy says. "I draw very sloppily because I don't just want to trace the projection. And then I work on that drawing." When working, he steadies his hand by holding it against the canvas. He often wears cotton gloves so that the rubbing motion won't hurt his hands. As he begins to refine the drawing, he likes to use a ruler and other tools such as a compass for precision.

Using a straightedge, or ruler, and a pencil, Roy refines his preliminary drawing.

He loves placing heavy black tape to simulate the black lines he will eventually paint on the canvas. He uses many different widths. "Sometimes I cut it and make my own sizes," he says. The tape can even be bent into curved shapes.

As he works, he may stick pieces of black tape on his hand. With his half glasses perched on the end of his nose, he stands up very close to the drawing. He may turn his head sideways or step backward to the end of the room to see what the painting looks like from different angles.

"Art is not just the technical part," Roy says. "Inside the artist there is a sense of how things should be placed. There is no rational way to explain that sense, but it guides where everything goes." If an artist tried to copy other artists' methods, he or she would not feel free to create, Roy cautions. Style and a sense of form are more important than the how-to. "But no one can

Roy places the black tape, which he cuts into special sizes and shapes.

possibly take a photograph of that," he says, laughing.

After working and reworking the drawing and establishing the shapes with black tape, he will simply start putting in colors. At this stage, he may tape paint samples to different areas of the drawing in order to get an idea of what the finished effect will be on a large scale. He'll try several different colors.

On a rack near a sink and an old desk are glass jars of thick, opaque paints: yellow, green, red, orange, silver, light violet, and many shades of blue. He is very particular that the paint be flat, or even-looking. He will apply several coats of paint so that there is no variation of color in any section. "I like the artificial quality, and that's part of the style I'm working in," he says. Roy notes

Roy mixes paints to precisely the color he wants. Pots of paint stand ready on the shelves.

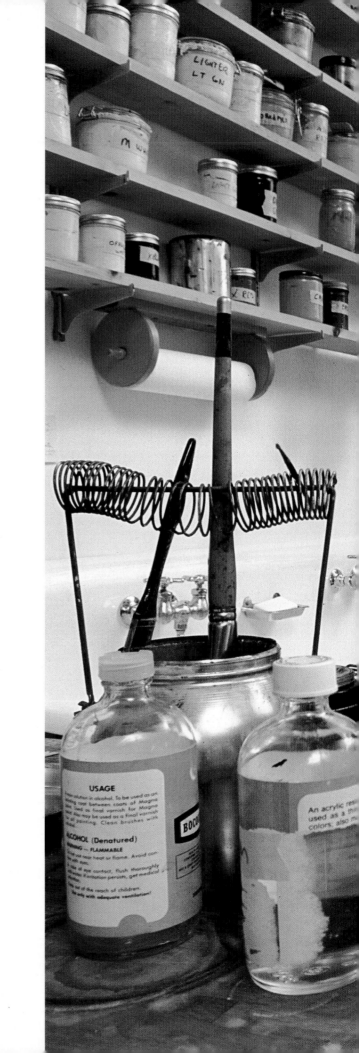

that it is harder to make all the parts of a painting look as if they belong in the same picture if there is no shading in the colors. He likes that challenge. The size and shape of the solid color patches become very important. Even the white areas are painted with three coats. Between each coat of paint, Roy applies varnish.

"With the use of dots, diagonals, and black paint, I have the kind of surface that I think can make interesting color combinations." He applies the dots with a stencil brush over a paper that has been perforated with holes. The diagonals are parallel strips of tape.

Roy's assistant Rob lifts masking tape with an X-Acto knife while Roy, below, paints.

12053

He is very interested in mechanical drawing, the work that draftsmen do, as well as in technical drawings done for catalogs and brochures, such as those for office equipment. The idea that some of his paintings look machine-made pleases Roy.

Many people immediately recognize Roy's work because of the Benday dots and heavy black diagonal lines that are his calling card. Whereas in the past, artists such as Van Gogh and Picasso would boldly emphasize their brushstrokes, Roy presents the entire painting without revealing any of the marks to us. The dots and diagonals give the painting what Roy calls an industrial texture. "It describes our age more," he says.

Precisely placed diagonals and patterns give this painting an industrial-age feeling.

Slats on the walls serve as floor-to-ceiling supports for the enormous *Interiors* canvases.

Because he does a series of paintings around a particular theme, such as house interiors, Roy tends to work on several paintings at once. Roy is in the middle of working on three very large *Interiors*. One is a living room. He has a smaller painting of a vase of flowers on a freestanding easel. He is deliberate and methodical in his work, but he can quickly change from one painting to the other as he gets inspired. He even paints the Oval Office of the White House.

What is unusual about these *Interiors* paintings is that there are no people. Although landscapes without human figures are common, it is rare to see paintings of so-called empty rooms.

These paintings are almost life-sized. "I realized the bigger they were, the more amusing they were," Roy says. He likes the idea that the sofa is large enough for someone to sit on, but that it looks so unreal no one would ever want to do so.

"I had done very large artist studio paintings," he says of the works he did in the style of the French painter Henri Matisse, who is famous for his lush colors and bold images. Several of Matisse's paintings depict models in rooms filled with decorative oriental rugs and flowers. Roy was also intrigued by technical drawings of office furniture and other rooms done by draftsmen.

There is a playful quality to Roy's work, and he likes to display things that amuse him around his studio. Pinned to a wall are instant photographs of him in funny poses—in one he's sticking out his tongue. He has clipped newspaper headlines such as "Jealous Computer Kills Top Scientist." On another wall is a label from a can showing a proud

Emeralds, 1961, has a fanciful quality.

**I Can See the Whole Room...
And There's Nobody in It!, 1961**

Sweet Dreams Baby!, 1965

green pelican. It reads: "King Pelican Vegetables."

His wit appears constantly in his artwork. One poster shows a man's head shaped like Swiss cheese. In another a finger is pointing straight out at the viewer. Roy draws objects we see in everyday life but that we take for granted. For example, he is very well known for his paintings of comic strip characters whose words in the bubbles above their heads sound almost foolish. "I don't care! I'd rather sink—than call Brad for help!" one blue-haired woman thinks, crying, as the waters of a river swirl around her head in a 1963 painting titled *Drowning Girl*. Another work, screen printed in 1966, shows a fist hitting a man with a big red "POW!" exploding from it. The man whose fist is connecting with the jaw cannot be seen. But there is a bubble that reads, "Sweet Dreams, Baby!"

Still another poster obviously refers to Roy himself. In it there's a blonde woman with tall buildings behind her. She is saying, "M-maybe he became ill and couldn't leave the studio!"

At his fingertips as he works, Roy has a rolling table with supplies such as masking tape and a feather duster. In a corner of the room there is a large rectangular mirror mounted on dolly wheels. Taped to it are pieces of painted paper, one with red stripes, the other flat orange.

He walks over to the easel that holds the picture of a vase of flowers. First, he erases a pencil mark and redraws it. He scrapes off some black tape with a razor blade. He adds more black tape. Next, he does something rather surprising. He loosens the large screws of the easel

Profile Head V, 1988, is a bronze sculpture of a woman.

and turns the canvas on its side. He continues working. Next, he tilts the vase the other way and works some more. Then he loosens the screws again to turn the painting diagonally. He walks up to examine his work, steps back, and squints at it.

Meanwhile, one of Roy's assistants, Rob, is working in another part of the studio, painting a section of the sofa as Roy has instructed him. Soon Roy will edge the heavy black tape with masking tape. Then he'll peel off the tape and begin painting the black lines.

Roy goes back to the big painting of a living room. It looks as if it could be any living room in America. That is Roy's intent. There are two hanging lamps, a sofa, a coffee table with flowers. On the wall behind the sofa is a painting of a table with two folding chairs—a painting within the painting. Roy has filled the larger painting with lots of diagonal black and white stripes. On the sofa there is a blue-and-white pillow.

He likes the shape of folding chairs. In his studio there is even a cutout of a folding chair on top of a filing cabinet.

Clearly he is passionate about being at work. He almost never takes a break. He doesn't like to repeat himself, and he is constantly looking for challenges. He likes to dare himself to do new things. He is always pushing the limits of his art.

Roy chooses another industrial-age pattern for the floor of this painting.

THE STUDIO

In some ways, Roy's studio resembles a carpenter's workshop or even a small storage warehouse. On one pegboard he hangs all sorts of tools: many kinds of saws, including a circular saw, as well as hammers, levels, and screwdrivers. Around the studio there are boxes of turpentine, marked "Highly Flammable." There are lots of packing materials, dollies for moving heavy objects, and dozens of rolls of paper towels. The acetylene torches and blue face masks painters must wear when the torches are lit lend a mysterious air. In the office, rows and rows of different sculptures, some encased in bubble wrap, stand at attention.

The phones ring often. The fax machine is constantly whirring with invitations for him to lecture or to attend gallery openings. The mail is thick with more of the same and with letters from people seeking his advice. He also receives many commissions to design artworks for a building or a town square.

***Archaic Head VI,
1989, bronze***

Surrounded by rolls of tape and his ladder, Roy searches for a drawing pencil.

Because of the constant interruptions, he must be very disciplined. He is at his studio each morning by nine, eats lunch at the same hour every day, and then often continues working until seven in the evening—or even later. Each time he is interrupted, he goes back to work immediately afterward. But one advantage of being an artist with a studio next to his home is that Dorothy, his wife, and other family members can come consult him on different matters at any time.

During the winters, he works in his studio in downtown New York. It is set up almost identically to his Southampton summer studio, although it is larger and has more space for storing his paintings and sculptures.

A quiet interlude as Roy examines his work.

THE IDEA

Many years ago, to amuse his children, Mitchell and David, Roy drew a Mickey Mouse cartoon. Something made him start thinking about using Mickey Mouse in some of his early artworks. By taking symbols from popular culture, he was trying to do exactly the opposite of the extremely abstract paintings that were popular at the time. Some abstract painters were using thick gobs of paint, and although you could see precisely where the brushstrokes were, it was nearly impossible for most people to see an object in those paintings. The paintings did not tell a story. Roy's work was a reaction to that. His paintings were clearly of specific everyday objects or familiar people and places. But he helped people see those things in very different ways. That's how Pop art was born: A British art critic devised that name for the style of artists such as Andy Warhol and Roy Lichtenstein because they used popular culture in their work.

Where do Roy Lichtenstein's ideas come from? Most artists seem to be at work—mentally—almost twenty-four hours a day. Even when he is reading the newspaper or looking through a catalog, Roy gets ideas. He is constantly refining his art.

"Usually an idea will pop into my mind while

Baked Potato, 1962

Roy repeatedly uses brushstrokes as a theme. *Red and White Brushstrokes, 1965.*

I'm working on another series," Roy says. "I won't quite see how to do it but it seems interesting. For example, in the early sixties I thought of painting a brushstroke. When I started to draw these brushstrokes, they looked like bacon. But they didn't look like brushstrokes! So part of the problem was how to make them look like brushstrokes. I wanted them to be artificial but not confused. And not as fussy as a real brushstroke might be if you photographed it. Then I found a way. At the very beginning I used India ink on acetate. The acetate repelled the ink and made a wonderful calligraphic brushstroke. When I projected it, interesting accidental things happened. It kind of had to rattle around in my brain for a while before I could figure out what it meant and what a painting should look like that had these brushstrokes in it. There's a learning process that goes on."

WHY IS IT ART?

What is clear is that Roy has carefully studied artists throughout the ages. Artists take what they have seen and refine it in order to make ideas and objects their very own.

Each time a person paints, Roy says, he is "learning something. It may just be sensitivity to that particular problem. It may be a question of the right color and the right place. Discipline and contrast. You are building some sort of pattern in your mind at the same time you're making art. It will be part of your experience for the next one that you do.

"It's rare that someone can do good art," Roy says, "but everyone who wants to should try. It's challenging and interesting. Without trying, you certainly can't achieve anything. The journey is worth taking no matter what the level of achievement. "

When Roy was still starting out in the 1960s, his work was often ridiculed by art critics. "Most people hated it," he explains straightforwardly. Yet it was a great period. "I was happy. Not because

The powerful painting, *Varoom!*, 1963, is an elaboration of a comic strip drawing.

they hated it! But there was a lot of controversy." He liked the liveliness of the discussions about his work. "Almost all the art critics and almost all the artists thought it was something horrible. They may be right!" he says with a smile. "Still, you don't love to read the reviews that are terrible. On the other hand, if you really believe in what you do, you don't believe the review!"

He had to persevere. "There are always little areas of doubt in your mind," he admits. "I think you should approach art as something you really love to do. That's the impulse. Otherwise, you'll never succeed in any way."

Creating art can be painstaking work. Roy emphasizes that "the journey is worth taking."

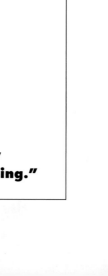

TECHNIQUES

Here are some of the various art techniques Roy uses in his work.

Gesso is traditionally a preparation of plaster of Paris and glue. Modern painters use an acrylic version. The purpose of gesso is to prevent the canvas from absorbing too much paint. It gives the canvas a uniform white appearance.

Magna is a type of acrylic paint. Roy likes to use Magna because it is easily removed with turpentine and because he feels it shows color better than many water-based acrylic paints.

For a *silk-screen print*, also known as a *serigraph*, an artist places a stencil on a stretched piece of silk. He puts paper underneath and then draws ink across the top of the silk with a squeegee—a kind of rubber-and-wood paddle.

A *woodcut* is a print made from a carved block of wood to which ink is applied.

Roy is touching up the painted diagonal lines with Magna and a paintbrush. He steadies the hand holding the brush by propping his left hand against the canvas.

SOME WELL-KNOWN

Image Duplicator, 1963
Magna on canvas

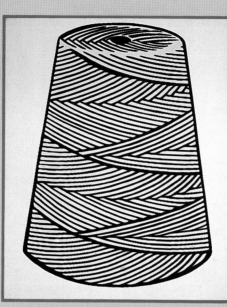

Large Spool, 1963
Magna on canvas

Explosion, 1965
Oil and Magna on
canvas

Cape Cod Still Life, 1973
Oil and Magna on canvas

Expressionist Head, 1980
Painted and patinated bronze

WORKS

Red Barn, 1969
Oil and Magna on canvas

Girl in Mirror, 1964
Enamel on steel

Indian Composition, 1979
Oil and Magna on linen

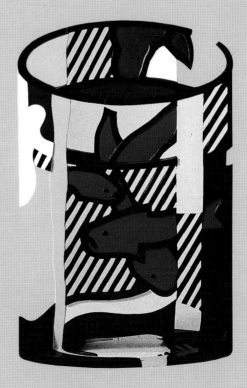

Goldfish Bowl II, 1978
Painted and patinated bronze

AN ART LESSON

Roy has always enjoyed teaching art classes because they give him an opportunity to stretch people's ideas about art. Here is an exercise Roy recommends to young artists to help set their imaginations free. Just as runners need to do sit-ups and pianists need to practice scales, artists need to do exercises to prepare to create. This is an excellent activity for loosening you up and helping your drawings be lively. It's also a way to keep your mind from taking charge of your drawing.

Get a piece of paper, a charcoal drawing pencil, and a slide projector. You will need to do this with a partner.

1. Set up the slide projector. Have your partner choose a slide—but don't let that person tell you what the image is. The slide should contain many objects.

2. Dim the lights.

3. Close your eyes while your partner projects the slide onto a screen or a wall. Ask him or her not to focus! The slide should be upside-down and as blurry as possible.

4. Open your eyes and draw what you see.

5. Have your partner sharpen the slide very gradually, over, let's say, a ten-minute period.

6. Keep going over your drawing until the slide is completely in focus. The result may be a messy drawing, but don't worry about that.

What do you think about the composition and feeling of your work?

ABOUT THE AUTHOR

LOU ANN WALKER is the author of the memoir, *A Loss for Words*, winner of the Christopher Award. Her book *Amy: The Story of a Deaf Child* was named a NCSS-CBC Notable Children's Trade Book in the Field of Social Studies. Regarding this book she says: "It was a joy for me to write about an artist whose work is so visual. Watching Roy in his studio provided me with fascinating glimpses into the creative process." Ms. Walker lives in Sag Harbor, New York, with her husband and daughter.

ABOUT THE PHOTOGRAPHER

An award-winning photojournalist, MICHAEL ABRAMSON has worked with *Newsweek*, the *New York Times*, *Life*, *Fortune*, and *Stern*. Abramson's books include *Amy: The Story of a Deaf Child* by Lou Ann Walker. He says: "Photographing Roy is not only a challenge but a privilege for a photographer. It is difficult because you have to wait very patiently in order to capture the gesture and nuance behind the technical aspects of Roy's work." Mr. Abramson lives in New York City.